INTRODUCTION TO MARKETING COMMUNICATION STRATEGY

JOHN LOK

ISBN 979-888606640-1

Contents

Preface *v*

Prologue *vii*

1. Marketing Communication Strategy Benefits And Functions 1

2. Learning Clever Shopping Consumer Mind 17

3. Exciting Salespeople Performance Methods 25

4. Property Seller Sale Skill Training 36

Preface

Introduction

The first chapter concerns to how to raise marketing communication channel methods to raise sale effort to any organizations. Why do organizations need have marketing communication strategy? What are the differences between owned marketing communication strategy organization and non oened marketing communication strategy organization? How can bring benefits if the organization has implemented marketing communication strategy? What are the weaknesses if the organization has not implemented marketing communication strategy?

In my this book, it has two parts. Part one explains what are marketing communication strategy functions and benefits. Part two indicate some case studies to explain how and why the industries need marketing communication strategy to be implemented in organizations.

This book second to four chapters indicate that why and how to raise sale communication channel methods to bring salespeople sale effort. When you are one salesperson, how you feel your boss is very kind to you or how you manage your salespeople when you are your sale team leader. Do you get compensation, when you help prior seller to promote his product? Do you get product return from prior sellers? Do you get cheque from your prior seller, after you pay cheque to the seller to buy the product? Do you choose K-Mart supermarket to shopping, if you own one supermarket? Had you been invited to be partner by one discounted supermarket? Do you prefer to choose to buy any products from internet from e-commerce influence? How to raise property sales agents sale effort after they are trained by sale communication skills . If you answer "NO" for all questions, you can not be one successful consumer because one successful consumer must have power to create income when they consume, such as " productive consumer".

This book will explain reasons how you can create wealth in consumption process when you need salespeople to help you to sell your products. Learning businessmen selling psychology, you are such as one intellent consumer to create wealth from them. I write this book aims to explain how and why you will have possible to become one wealth clever consumers in nowadays social consumption model. I shall give opinions to explain what advantages that why and how marketing communication strategy will bring to any organization after it had implemented to let readers to know. This book can teach students and marketing practicers to increase marketing communication knowledge and concept how to apply to any organizations in order to achieve sale growth and build consumer positive emotion to choose to buy the brand's product or consume service.

Prologue

Table of content

Chaper 1
Marketing communication
strategy benefits and functions

- What are marketing communication strategy benefits? p. 4-10
- Marketing communication functions
- Marketing communication case studies applying

- The possible sale of relationship marketing and communication in public utility service p.11-20

- Understanding food industry marketing communication (pull marketing communication strategy) p.21-30

- The role of marketing communication strategy in theatre management

- Marketing communication function in clothing industry (push marketing communication strategy) p.31-40

Chapter 2
Learning clever shopping consumer mind

- Is productive consumption the best wealth accumulative method p.41-51

Chapter 3
How to create the bottom of the pyramid to the low income level consumer consumption desire p.52-65

- Exciting salespeople performance methods

● How salespeople behaviors influence consumer psychology and behavioral relationship

Chapter 4

Property seller sale skill training

Explaining clear property buyer contract agreement requirement

● Is a "Default" Defined in the Sales Contract? p.66-75

● How is a Breach of a Sales Contract Settled?

● Advertisement Property channels choice

CHAPTER ONE

Marketing communication strategy benefits and functions

What are marketing communication
strategy benefits?

Can marketing communication strategy help organizations to build brands, innovation, developing relationship, create good consumer service and communication benefit. Most marketing professionals believe effective communicaton strategy can help organizations to raise brand competition as well as to create and enhance relationship with consumers and other stakeholders. Marketing communication strategy is concept of communication through the promotional mix, with these better-educated, cost-conscious and demanding customers.

Why do organizations need marketing communication strategies? Marketing communication strategy is concept used for sales promotion, product publicity, events sponsorships and direct marketing. It can help new brands to raise familiarity to let customers to know when the brand product plans to enter the marketing to sell in beginning.

Nowadays, organizations need promotional mix strategy to let consumers to familiar their new products, such as public relations, marketing, advertising, promotion and online media. Generally, organizations expect to achieve these aims. Otherwise, one effective marketing communication strategy can assist the organizations to drive forces for growth.

The driving forces include: Value of money means the organizations want to gain maximum value for money with maximum impact, resulting in raising value of money to different products in different departments and pressure on margins: Increasing pressure on organizations' bottom lines means organizations seek compensatory savings in all activities through saving, economic pressures and profitability, increasing client confidence means specially to understand retailers, cutomers and an increased confidence in using other marketing communication disciplines, a dissatisfaction with advertising means resulting in clients using other disciplines to improve consumer relations and sales, increasing mass media costs means where database costs decreased, mass-media costs (especially television, increased dramatically) and a reduction advertising agencies expenses in terms of strategic input and direction. Hence, one effective marketing communication strategy can be possible to assist the organizations to reduce advertising expense, raise brand familiarity, increase client number, raise product sale price for long term benefits.

Some marketing professional researches recommend marketing communication strategy ought have these several stages, they include as below:

Stage one is tactical coordination of marketing communication. It means to find what are the fails on function areas including advertising, promotion, direct response, public relation and special events. The tactical coordination of marketing communication strategy aims to find why a high degree of interpersonnal and cross-functional communications needed as formal policies and procedures are insufficient to achieve the organization marketing communication operation. It aims to find what the weaknesses are to cause the organization's internal communication between different departments and external communiation to its clients inefficience and ineffectiveness.

Stage two is refining the scope of marketing communication. The organization begins to examine communication from the consumer's viewpoint, include all contact and entry points between the organization and clients. The scope of communication activities also include internal marketing to employees, suppliers and other business partners.

The entensive information on consumers is gathered through primary and secondary market research as well as actual consumer behavior data and feedback channels are created to gather information about consumers. So, it aims to find what marketing communication challenges influence the organizations' internal and external communication difficulties to influence poor unsatisfactory customer behavior peformance to seek valuable solution to raise the organization's internal and external marketing communication more efficient and effective to raise customer communication success.

Then, third stage concerns how to improve and apply skill to build good marketing communication channel. Due to the marketing communication strategy implementation organization will need to learn how to use data obtained through IT skill to provide a basis for the identification of values and to monitor the impact of integrated internal and external marketing communication programmes over time. So, IT must be incorporated effectively into communication planning development and execution.

The final stage is financial and marketing communication strategic integraton. It emphasizes shifts from skills and data to driving corporate strategic planning using consumer information and insight. Financial measures should be adapted into the evaluation process based on return on consumer investment measures.

So, these stages will be the key compenent to raise or improve the external marketing communication efforts with the internal marketing communication efforts to raise the overall organizational corporate brand for long term effective and internal and external marketing communication channels to employees and consumers both stakeholders' benefits.

Marketing communication functions

Why do organizations need marketing communication? What are marketing communication functions to organizations? What kinds of challenges will encounter if the organization lacked an efficient marketing communication strategy? This chapter will be explained above these questions clearly.

Marketing communication seems to be gathered information and communication seems to be gathered information and communication technology, which will influence every aspect of consumer need in order to bring positive or negative emotions to the brand of product. Hence, if the organization had effective marketing communicaton tools and strategies, which will raise its competitive effort in nowadays business societies.

An effective marketing communication strategy or tool will help the brand of product to build good emotion to its consumers. The steps include: The organization needs have one good marketing plan. Then, it needs to design the right or suitable kind of marketing strategy to satisfy its products or services characteristics. Finally, if its marketing communication tools or methods are suitable to the organization to be used to promote. Then, it will either build good brand or remember or familiar as well as build either good (positive) or bad (negative) emotion to the customers. So, it seems an efficient and marketing communicatin tool or method will help the organization to increase customer familiarity and build positive emotion to its product or service. Otherwise, an inefficient marketing communication tool or method will not help the organization to increase customer familiarity build negative emotion to its product or service. So, it is one important function to any marketing communication strategy.

Why organizations ought need to spend time and human resource / communication tool resources to design the most right or the most suitable marketing communication strategy for its organization to promote its product or service? Before any organizatins design any communication strategy , they need to know what is this marketing suitation. In general, marketing is defined the establishment of mutually satisfying exchange relationships between the brand's product or/and service and its clients. It is managing profitable client relationships. It's goal of marketing is to attract new clients by promising superior value and to keep and grow current clients by delivering satisfaction.

Therefore, the marketing function is to identify client needs and to provide a product or service that meets some or all of those needs, accessibily and at an acceptable price to the target market. Hence, the organization's marketing communication strategy is only one part of its overall marketing strategy. A marketing strategy includes how to help the organization to promote its product or service, how to sell its product or provide its service, how to arrange the reasonable price strategy, how to help the organization to improve production and distribution efficiencies, how to focus on continue product improvement, how to focus on aggregive selling tactics, focuses on customer needs, applied on integrated marketing approach, how to give welfare of society.

How does the marketing communication strategy influence the overall marketing strategy success to the organization? An effective marketing communication strategy can create value for customers and build good customer relationship for the brand of product or service. It's function includes that is can let the organization understands markplaces and its customer needs and want more clearly, it can assist the organization how to design a customer-driven marketing strategy if the organization can build good relationship between them , it can also help the organization to construct a marketing communication strategy(program) that delivers superior value. Then, when the organization has an efficient marketing communication strategy, it can help the organization to build relationship and create customer delight in long term. Finally, it can help the organization to achieve a superior capture value from its clients to create profits and client quality more easily.

Why do organizations need have an efficient marketing communication strategy? The reasons include that as below:

In fact, customers have much choices, usually different product or service marketing places will have (excess) oversupply of product or service to influence consumers to make careful choices to buy which brand of product or consume service in whose choice processes. So, if the brand of product or service cn build good communication relationship between itself and customers. It can influence customers to have positive emotion to choose to buy its product or consume its service. So, any organizations needs have good price, location (place), people (staff) strategies, it also need have good promotion (communication) strategy in order to learn how to communicate to its customers to keep close relationship and build positive emotion to let them to feel.

However, the marketing communication amix must include these several tools for any organizations to choose which kind(s) of communication tool(s) is (are) the best tool(s) in order to be used to promote its clients efficiently. They include: Advertising, it means that controlled paid for communication, it consists of communication messages, initiated by a specific communicator in the mass media to a defined target audience. Personal selling involves interpersonal communication between sellers and buyers through personal interactions. Sales promotion concerns the free and favorable exposure of a product's benefits or value in the media, public relations can establish and maintain favorable relations between an entity and its stakeholders. So, any organization needs to choose either only use one kind of communication tool or more than one kind of communication tools in order to achieve an efficient marketing communiation strategy to build positive emotion and good product or service image or familiar brand to let its potential customers to know by any above one media. Also, it implies that customers won't know or familiar to the brand more clearly if the organization had not implement any promotion tool(s) to promote its pooduct or service to letits clients to know whether its existing product or service can give what benefits to them.

How to achieve an efficient marketing communication strategy? To achieve an efficient marketing communication strategy to the organization. It includes this process: It needs to identify who are its target customers (main target customer) potential customer and prospects. Then, it needs to measure the valuation of its different groups of client (e.g. age, sex, shopping characteristics). Next, it needs to create and deliver the right or suitable or useful or persuasive messages and incentives to let its different group clients to know wha its product or service existing in its country or globale market places. Next, it needs to estimate how much it can earn return on its customer investment for its future possible reward. Because it if estimated that its marketing communication expenditure can not achieve its budget return in customer investment reward. Then, it needs revise its this (these) kind of marketing communication tool (s) whether it (they) is (are) useful to promote its product or service to let clients to know. Finally, it needs to implement its budgeting allocation and evaluation to review its every time marketing communication tool(s) whether is (are) achieved its original aim. If it believed or confirmed its slae result is not successful. Then, it needs to revise its marketing communication tool(S) whether they (it) is (are) the most suitable or useful one tool(s) t be used to promote to its clients in the future. Hence, the whole process of marketing communication strategy is very important to influence its sale number. Every product or service provider needs to spend enough time and human resource to marketing communication tool resources to decide how to design to implement in order to sell in failure finally.

For one integrated marketing communication model of brand contact delivery system case example: The brand;s customer (proposect exposure will include message and incentive both aspects. Message and incentive will bring promotin communication informations concern relevance and receptivity to the brand's product or service to let its customers to know or remember or familiar by these any one or more than one delivery systems , such as product/use of the package product message tool or directed marketer channel or undirected member channel or traditional media tools (accesses or unintentional , such as TV, radio, magazine, signage outdoor direct marketing tool or electronic media tools (wired or wireless) such as website second intranet or mobile phone engins GPS or special events promotion methods (natural or sponsored) , such as holiday events or sport cultural trade events. All any one of these media delivery systems will be one choice tool to let the product/ service providers to be choosed to find which tool is the most efficient delivery tool. Hence, one marketing communication strategy elements include the marketing communication source is the company/brand or agency, the brand message concerns (planned , unplanned, product or/and service) and the channel includes newspapers, TV, radio, magazine, e-mails, salespeople sale service, customer service, internet and the receiver is the target audience in the whole marketing communication process. Finally, the delivery system will bring feedback to the company/brand, agency and the target audience both. The feedback includes that purchase/not purchase, request information, visit store, sample product, repeat visit/purchase.

Consequently, any marketing communication strategy will bring feedback to let the product/service provider to know in order to judge or predict whether its potential customers will have positive or negative emotion (attitude) to choose to buy its product or consume its service. Thus, feeback affect will be one important factor to influence the product or service providers success. If the product / service providers and clients both feedback trends to more negative emotion to its potential customers, then it can attempt to follow whose ideas to find what internet weaknesses or external threats to cause whose potential customers feel negative emotion to its product or/and service. Then, it can attempt to find solutions to avoid whose negative emotion is caused more easily. Thus, an efficient marketing communication strategy can help the product/service provider how to raise its potential clients' emotion to be trended more positive emotion for their product or service choices.

The possible sale of relationship marketing and communication in public utility service

What are the function of marketing communication to public utility service ? If the public utility service orgnizaton lacks an efficient communication channel between internal staffs and utility consumers, what kinds of challenges who will encounter. How to they make solution ? What are the negative attitude of the utility consumers will be if it lacked an efficient communication service between them?

In fact, many countries‘ public utility service is monopoly market. Their governments ususally have a regulated prices to control their price to be charged to public utility consumers. Consumers have had affordable public utility access to these utility service, but they have been defenceless against the service providers . Hence , every government usually control utility service providers' price charged behavior in order to avoid their excess of charge. So, publis utility service providers have realized that those is a competition on the utility service market.

Hence, an effective and efficient marketing communication channel will bring those benefits ot advantages between the organization's internal staffs and every utility service consumer. I shall indicate the advantages as below:

Firstly, an efficient marketing communicatin channel can let utility service consumers to feel whether the public utility service is a real public service. Due to public utility service aims to provide any enough utility remains to consumers to use, such as electricity , water, gas, oil etc. is the field on non-business marketing because the public utility service providers do need aim on profit seeking . This is made characteristics as well by the fact that in many service field, e.g. higher education, public transport, public utility service. So , an efficient communication marketing channel can let the public service consumersm who can make easy to distinct between public and private as well as between profit and non profit , e.g. the students can judge whether their schools charge higher education fee or lower education fee in the general school fee charge level and judge whether the public transport charges higher or lower transport for general public transport service standard charge level and judge whether the gas, oil, water, electricity utility service charge is accepted to general public utility service charge standard level. Hence, an efficient marketing communication channel can let the public service consumers have more familiar and effort to judge whether the public service providers' charge is reasonable.

However, an efficient communication marketing channel is very important to assist the public utility service consumers to make a distinction as well . Every public utility service organization has responsibility to let public service consumers to know what are basic services to be provided to let them to judge whether the kind of possibility of public service substitution is small or large to let the publis service consumers to choose in the country 's current public service market to let them to judge whether the public service quality is good or bad and whether the price conditions are reasonable. Hence, an efficient marketing communication channel can build the good relationship between the public service organization and its public service consumers.

Do public utility services have important characteristics from marketing communication channel? It is agreed that efficient marketing communication channel is needed to any public utitlity service industries. It has chose marketing and communication relationship to any public utility service orgnizations. It is to think in terms of back office organizations in most person to person contact based services, but in the case of the utility services, the situation is unique different. In fact, the role of back office is significant different in the case of public utility services. In general , public utility consumers do not assess the work of background staff as they are unseen and are not usually part of the service providing process. However, the result of the servicing activity depends on the work of the back office. So, it explains that why efficient internal department communication is very important beween public utility service back office staffs. There is no effective public utility service without the tools, equipment and operating staff and the application of efficient and effective communication relationship marketing is challenges by this fact. For example, the role of power , heating, water and long distance telephone supply etc. customer service front office staff role is influential to their service efficiency by the back office staffs cooperation. If they have good communication channel to let them to work in order to achieve efficient communication effect. Then, the front office public utility service staffs can provide better consumer service to satisfy any public utility service consumer needs or build the high direct consumer service relationships between them.

Besides, efficient communication marketing strategy can assist the public utility service organization to promote its prices to let public utility service consumers to feel more acceptable to the price level chrge range. It is often difficult for service providers to apply differentiating price strategies and to use prices as promotional devices. Even, when price incentives are allowed public utility service providers rarely use. There effectively with elements of the marketing mix or with effective segmentation program to an efficient communication marketing strategy can help any public utility service organizations to solve any tangible and/or intangible communication challenges, such as back office and front office staffs communication challenges, fron toffice customer service staffs poor or inefficient service performance challenge, who causes utility service consumers to feel emotion unsatisfactory or do behavioral complains. So, effective communication marketing strategy is important tool to influence any public utility service organizations successes.

Understanding food industry marketing communication (pull marketing communication strategy)

In food industry , it needs have an efficient marketing communication strategy in order to the food providers can persuade their food consumers to choose to buy their food easily. Firstly, the food provider needs to understand the global consumer's prefence to find how any why to persuade they to choose to buy their food products. It is important to develop marketing communication strategies to solve challenges and find or seek opportunities in the communicaion process between the food providers (manufacturers) and its food retailers, food wholesalers (supermarkets , food stores). In its communication marketing strategy, it needs to consider two channels: The first channel is supply chain development and management channel. The food supplier (manufacturer) needs to learn how to manage its differene kinds of food supply chain, learn how to manage its food quality and food transportation logistics methods and learn how to communicate to its food retailers or food wholesalers how to help it to sell its different kinds of food to let consumers to buy attractively. The another channel is that it needs to learn how drive food consumer behavioral consumptionand learn hoe to predict why whose consumption behavioral change. Hence, the food supplier (manufacturer) needs to learn how to communicate with its food retailers and food wholesalers to know how any why its food consumers' choices to but its foods behavioral change. It concerns that it needs to communicate with them to learn how and why its old food consumers‘ taste change, researchs and builds new food product brand development as well as learns how to achieve efficient marketing communication strategy and point of sale strategies. Finally, the food supplier) manfacturer) will gather all data from there both channels to brings all data together to implement strategy revisited and revised the weaknesses and keep strengths in order to find the most useful solvable method to attract new potential food consumers to choose to buy to food or keep its old consumers to continue to choose to buy its food. Hence, one efficient marketing communication strategy which can represent the " PROMOTION" element of the marketing mix. Such on this food industry case, food marketing is all about food selling and communicating ideas be they to buy a good taste of food or good food salespeople service or take notice of a publis health apeal (e.g. eat fruit and vegetabl). None of this is possible without a good and effective communication strategy between the food supplier (manufacturer) and its food retailers or food wholesalers.

In many food and agricultural markets, the food and agriculture suppliers (producers and supply chain/ channel partners, it has become increasingly difficult to differentiate between food or agricultural product offerings. So, the number of available and visable positioning opportunities also diminishes. So, it implies that efficient communication strategy can assist them to create long-life marketing communication opportunities to promote their any agriculturl food success. Some of the key roles that promotion can play in food marketing include as below:

An efficient communication marketing strategy can help the agricultural food producers to build brand depth awareness. For example, when some food consumers ask the supermarket staffs concern which brands of chicken taste taht they can choose to buy in the supermarket chilled meat sections. If the chicken food supermarket staffs can speak some brands of chicken food, e.g. steggles, lillydale, ingham etc. brands. Then, the supermarket staffs can help those chicken brand producers to promote the different chicken taste food to let the supermarket consumers to know. So, it means that the brand of chicken food producers can build good communication relationship to the supermarket . Then, the supermarket staff's promotin behavior , it seems to advertise the chicken food producers to let the supermarket customers to know or be familiar the brand of chicken's different chicken tastes.

So, good food taste marketing communication strategy can achieve good or phycial availability , such as the food producers can arrange how much different food distribution to different wholesalers or retailers, such as supmarkets, food stores. Hence, if they had good communication relationship, whose middle sale agents, such as supermarkets or food stores will tell about how much different kinds of food will encounter food shortage or food excess perishable challenges in next month in order the food producers can predict who ought continue to increase supply the kind of food or reduce supply for every kind of food to the supermarkets or food stores to help them to sell next month. It aims to achieve all food will be fresh and good quality to provide to food buyers to eat. So, predicting food supply number will be one important solution to food perishable challenge.

In conclusion,an efficient marketing communication stragegy can assist the agricultural food producer to avoid to supply the excess of different kinds of food number or the shortage of different kindsof food number challenge. If the agricultural foos producers can build good marketing communication relationship between itelf and its food wholesalers/ food retailers, e.g. supermarkets, food stores. Then, the foor producers will have goos notice about its different kinds of food sale number data every month or every week ,even every day in order to decide whether it ought increase or decrease how much accurate predictive number of the kind of food to its food retailers or wholesalers to sell every day to avoid the different kinds of food excess or shortage challenges. So, efficient marketing communiation strategy is very serious to agriculturing food producers.

The role of marketing communication strategy
in theatre management

Why does theatre industry need communication media, e.g. combination of advertisement, publicity, and public relation, plus other marketing tools in promotional activities of theatre management strategy. If the theatre performance provider neglected to achieve efficient marketing communication strategy , it will bring what kinds of challenges to influence performance entertainment consumers' entertainment desires.

Threatre industry can be explained to refer to any structure or group of people (even non professonal existing primarily for the preparation/ presentation of theatrical performance, such as dance, music, song, movie, life show etc. performance for purpose of audience entertainment activities, such as movie is one kind of popular entertainment in threatre industry. It can provide entainment activity to entertain audience to satisf their visible enjoyable desires when they had bought tickets to choose any movies to watch in theatres.

What is the purpose of communication marketing management principles and strategies to threatrical procedures? Theatrical communication marketing management strategy consists planning, staffing, organizing , motivating, directing and controlling human and material resourcesin the arts of the theatre and their interaction in order to attain the predetermined objectives of guaranteeing satisfaction and maximizing profit. So , theatrical organization needs have efficient communication between its internal departments as well as itself and its any performance entertainment service providers . It aims to achieve every final entertainment performances which can be more attractive to let audiences enjoy to watch or listen any kinds of entertainment performances.

What role is a directing communication channel to threatre industry? Advertising is the structured and composed non-personal communication of information ususally paid for and usually persuasive in nature about products, services and ideas by identified sponsors through various media. Advertising can be explained the techniques and practices used to bring products , services , opinions or causes to public notice for the purpose of persuading the public to respond what is advertised. It seems theatre industry needs have efficient communication to let internal departments or entertainment performance service providers to communicate to them to achieve to prepare any attractive advertisments before any entertainment performance implementation. Because if one entertainment performance provider can provide attractive advertisements can persuade and notify potential audiences to choose to buy tickets to enter threatres to watch the entertainment performance service provider's any entertainment performance event more easily. So, the threatre service provider and its entertainment performance srvice providers need have good communication in order to advertise every different kind of entertainment performance event more attractive to let its audiences to feel. So, theatre provider needs to concern this internal and external communication issue in order to apply advertisement promotive channel to attract potential audiences.

Other kind of promotion channel to theatre providers. It is publicity , it is difference to public relations or even advertisement. Although, publicity seems a tool of public relations, but the aim of publicity is to create awareness through the media by placing news information about on organization, such as the threatre provider and its entetainment performance service providers. The major characteristic of publicity that differentiates it from other marketing tools is tat it is not be paid for by an identified sponor . Otherwise, public relation serves mainly the create an understanding between the threatre entertainment performance service provider and its publics (audiences) , thereby creating awareness for its entertainment performances. A public relations campaign takes various forms. It can be through the threatre provider's sponsorship of programmes beneficial to the audiences or through the award of scholarships is through any music, song, movie, dance, life show etc. different kinds of entertainment performance projects that attempt to build better understanding between the theatre provider and its audiences . So, having taken a critical look of advertising , publicity and public relations will be the important part of communication or promotion tools in theatre industry.

The aim of every well communiation methods to manag threatre , which can have much influential to impact audiences' emotions and their entertainment performance consumption desires to the theatre provider. However, the marketing communication channel of advertisement has weakness to theatre entertainment performance service provider, it depends on most printing spending times, as the printing of posters. This is not out of place because it has its role to play in marketing , but the fact, the electronic media advertisement does not need to print papers . Hence, this kind of promotion method will bring more economic benefit to the theatre service and entertainment performance service provider both.

A theatre entertainment performance provider will have different departments to cooperate efficiently in order to prodices theatrical performances, such as drama, dance, movie, opera, music , life show etc. entertainment performances. So, one department of any theatre provider needs t make uss of advertisement to create awareness about their any entretainment performance to any let audiences (entertainment consumers)to know. So, efficient communication is necessary between the threatre provider's departments.

In conclusion, in theatre entertainment performance industry, any theatre entertainment performance providers expect their every movie, song, mucis, dance, life show etc. art performances can be promoted from advertisement , publicity and public relations marketing tools successfully. In efficient marketing communication strategy is an essential facility available to every internal departments in order to strengthened cooperation how to design every advertisement, publicity and public relations channel to let every different kinds of art performance to be promoted to attract potential audiences to choose to bu admission tickets to watch or listen the theatre entertainment performances more easily.

Marketing communication function in clothing industry

What marketing communication tools are the most useful or suitable to clothing industry? I shall indicat mailings, telephones and personall interview marketing communicatiot ools to reflect the useful function to clothing industry.

Nowadays, clothing fashion products total change of market had changed rapidly and its new trends which has changed too rapidly suddenly after 1950 year. So, the different brands of clothing products need to be designed unique to satisfy clothing buyer individual specific groups and / or lifestyle needs. Also, the different design of fashion clothing products can represent every different clothing brand's image. However, sufficient promotin will be one influential tool to help the clothing product designer to promote is any kinds of cloths to let potential cloth clients to know or help it to build familiar brand image in the clothing market.

Good fashion design can challenge conventional views. It should be recognized their consumers very in the conservation they have towards fashion styles and also speed and readiness with which change their opinions. So, an efficient marketing communication strategy will let the clothing products designer to gather whose cloth clients' opinions in order to predict how they ought to decide to design preferable fashion styles choices more easily in order to let it it follow general clothing product buyers' fashion styles design choice to design many attractive fashion styles of clothing products to let them to persuade them to choose to buy its clothing products more easily.

So, clothing buyer personal interviews or telephone individual contact or posting mail questionnaire enquiry promotion method will be one suitable to be used to promote in clothing industry. Because these markeing communication tools can gather any clothing buyer individual opinions in order to help the designers to understand. Then, clothing marekt can enhance the clothing design creating process and marketing personnel appreciate that within the fashion industry design can lead as well as respond to customer requirements progress can be made more easily. Thus, telephone, clothing buyers individual intervew or questionnaire researching or post mailing questionnaire researching marketing communication tools will have effort to help the bradn of clothing designer to predict how to design its cloths styles which can persuade potential clothing buyers to choose to buy its brands of any kinds of styles clothing products to wear more easily in possible. So, any clothing designer needs have a fashion marketing concept and have demonstrated equal concern for design, customers and profits. Thus, any clothing designer's marketing communication strategy needs to concentrate on fashion design promotion. It means that when the clothing product provider has good different styles of clothing design products and the suitable place(clothing stores) and the reasonable price setting , then it needs have good promotion (communication tool) e.g. telephone, TV, radio, magazine etc. to its target audience (e.g. child, young , old age , expensive or cheap clothing product buyer group, traditional design or popular fashion design style clothing product preference cloth buyers.

Nowadays, clothing communication medias include broadcast advertisement (TV and radio), print advertisement (magazines and newspapers), brochures and booklets, posters and packaging, motion pictures, directories, display signs and symbols and logoes. Any one of these communication medias can help any clothing designers to build its brand to be familiar to let its potential buyers to know. Instead of these communication media, sales promotion is usuall connect closely with adventing in clothing industry. The basic types of sales promotion include coupons, samplying , refunds and rebates, premiums and gifts , games, contexts. Any onf od these sale promotion will be one good communication method to persuade the clothing buyers to choose to attempt to buy the brand of any styles of clothing products tpo wear more easily. The primary communication objectives of these tools ususally are: stimulation of clothing consume trials, increase of rebuy rates and reward of loyal customers in order to fasten he selling process. However, promotion should bot be used as an ongoing program, as it is only a short term tastic. Otherwise, it can easily lower the price of the brand of clothing products.

The another kind communication tool is public relations, it means to build good relations with the clothing provider to public by obtaining favorable publicity. The " publics" are a the clothing provider's stakeholder, such as suppliers, employees, customers or governments, public relations activities can include press relationships, sponsorships, product placement, events management and crisis management. So, good public relation can help the clothing provider to build good brand image to let clothing buyers to know or familiar.

The final communication media is personal selling. It involves face-to-face activities, the clothing provider's clothing sales representatives of a particular clothing brand with the aim to inform, persuade or remind a clothing buyer to take appropriate action. The most common examples of personal selling include: sales presentations, sales meetings, incentive programs, samples, fairs and trade shows.

Consequently, any one of above communication medias will bring benefits to the clothing provider. However, the clothing provider needs to spend time and human resource and promotion communication tools resource to implement one effective marketing communication stragtegy to help its hw to promote its clothing products to let its potential clients to be familiar its different kinds of styles cloths more attractively. So, it seems on efficient communiation strategy can help the clothing provider to raise its different kinds of clothing design to attract its clothing buyers' consideration more easily.

CHAPTER TWO

Learning clever shopping consumer mind

Any one customer hopes to create wealth from consumption process. I believe that it is possible to achieve or implement this goal . You need to remember that your consumption behaviors can not help you to create wealth, if you can change your consumption attitude or mind how to become one clever consumption. It is possible to help you to save much money or wasting money to consume in long time accumulative consumption time.

Do you feel that one cheap or discount price product? It must be attractive and it is right or suitable to you to choose to buy to compare other no discount or more expensive similar products in nowadays market. Do you feel that you may use the cheap or discount product for long time to compare other similar, but no discount or much expensive products? For example, you can use this cheaper product for one year maximum, but if you buy another " no discount" similar product, you can guarantee to use at least five years.

So, when you use the cheaper product after one year. You need to pay extra money to buy another product to replace it, if it is one essential product. It means that you must need to buy another similar product to replace it. If you still buy discount or cheap the kind of similar product every year. Moreover, the kind cheap and discount product price assumes to raise 10% at least every year. Do you feel that your actual expenditure will stable increase, when you must need to buy the kind of discount product to use every year? Otherwise, if you decide to choose to buy the much expensive producty before, you won't need to spend extra money to buy the kind of similar product every year, because this " no discount" product can guarentee to satisfy your need to use at least five years. So, one clever consumer won't only consider whether the product has how much discount, wo will consider whether how long its actual useful time.

In the discount shop businessmen beneficial view point, he will have role if he still sell discount, but no long useful time products to his clients, because if the clients discover his all any discount products must not be used longer time to compare the other competitors, they sell more expensive, but longer time durable similar quality and appearance products. Then, the discount shop businessmen may face lose old clients consumption risk again, if they don't calculate the discount benefit, they begin to calcualte useful durablr time benefit. So, he needs to solve this " discount product short durable time"challenge, if he hopes his old client number won't be lose.

This case brings one question: How you , such this discount shop businessman's consumer and this discount shop owner can create wealth together? I have one co-operative partnership form method to help you to create wealth? So, you won't feel buy its any discount products to bring money loss in long time as well as this discount shop businessman can still keep his old clients in possible. When you are this discount shop partners. You can buy any one kind of discount product, but you can also earn income and build asset in the same time. I believe that you won't choose any shops to buy similar products , and you will continue to buy any discount products, even you feel that they may only be used short time from your co-operative discount ship because when you are this shop partner, after you sell any products, then you can earn each product income and raise your any fixed assets value from this ship, such as this shop market value, product market value, office market value, furniture and office equipment market sold value, even this shop's goodwill (intangible asset market value). So, you will create wealth when you are this shop's partner, you can earn share any one product profit and share this shop's any tangible and intangible asset value, when you and your partner to close this shop in future one day. You can share this shop's all goodwill and product ans office, store market value to earn accumulative wealth in your shop future one closing day.

Even, you both can help your new clients to co-operate to do this shop's business togethe. When any one client buys your shop's any one kind of product, your every client can be your client member, if he/she recommend your any kind of discounted product to his/her friends or families to choose to buy your shops's any one kind of product in success. Then, your clients can earn commision for every product, it's recommend from your clients' introduction. So, you do not need to spend much expensive any advertisement expenditure to promote your products, because your clients will attempt to help you ro recommend any one kind of product to their friends ot families to buy, after they use the kind of product , they know what characteristics and feature the kind of product owns, then they have confidence to help you to sell your any kinds of this discounted shop products to their friends or families in success, because your clients can become your sellers to hope to earn extra commission for every product.

In conclusion, although this discounted shop owner may face old client long durable time confidence loss risk, but if he can choose to share every product sale profit and this discounted shop's fixed and intangible (goodwill) asset future market value benefit to you, such as partner as well as selling commission benefit to your future every new client after their verbal prouct recommendations attract their potential families and friends to be persuaded to buy your both partners' any kind of products successfully. So, you and this discounted owner can be one partnership relationship, you will prefer to buy this discounted shop's any kinds of products, because you can earn long term profit and asset market value from your partner a well as you can increase much confidence to persuade your friends and families to buy your any kinds of products after you attempt to use any kinds products of your discounted ship. Moreover, when you can recommend to your friends and families to buy this discounted shop's any kinds of products, then you can also earn commission , even your friends and families can help you to earn commisson when they can recommend to any one to buy your discounted products successfully and their all families and friends relationship consumers will help you to bring extra commission income . So, your commission income is no limit, its only increases, but it does not reduce. Hence, it explains why that you can be one productive power consumer when you choose to be partner to this discounteed shop owner, due to your every time consumption, you can earn every time profit from this discounted shop partner.

Anyway, it means that you can choose to cooperate to other " no discount" or " no cheaper" businessmen to be partners to share their profit, and commission when you consume their products, but you can also bring productive profit as the same time. It is one good consumer productive wealth psychological sale method.

Is productive consumption the best wealth accumulative method

What are the differences between general consumers and productive consumers ? Similarly, general consumer means that any buyers need to spend money to choose to buy any kinds of products. Otherwise, productive consumers mean that any buyers need to spend money to choose to buy any kinds of products as the same time. So, productive consumers will have possible to earn no limited income after they choose to buy the preference of products.

I shall indicate some kinds of products or investment, they may help consumers to bring extra income in possible. For share investment behavioral market example, in general, share buyers will accept to pay the acceptable share price to choose to buy the company's shares, if they felt that the company's share price will rise up later. Share market buyer is good example of productive consumer because he will earn more income if he invests the share, its price can raise up absolutely. If he has accurate insight to judge the company's share price will rise up how long time and when its price will fall down. Then, he will decide to buy many number of shares to wait the company's nest time share falling down period comes back again. So, he will attempt to spend little time, e.g. one to two hours per day to gather data concerns this company's past share price variation , e.e. what level is its share price the highest and the lowest changes, how long it can keep its share price changes. Every day, his analysis will help him to increase confidence to predict when this company's share pice will rise up the highest level. Then, he may decide final share purchase decision to choose to buy this company's shares. If he chooses ten companies‘ shares to buy, he can have more than five companies' shares price rise up. Hence, he may be one successful productive consumer.

For another property market example, some property buyers can be successful property productive consumers, because they can predict that their property investment price will rise up. Because they accept to spend little time, e.g. one to two hours per day to compare where property location and property design and property quality whether it can satisfy the property buyer's comfortable feeling to live. All of different property price data needs to be gathered in order to make accurate prediction where property price will rise up more in the future. Then, he will have confidence to choose to buy the property to live. If the property price can real rise up, then he is one successful productive consumer.

As these two kinds of property product and share investment example, the productive consumers have these characteristics. They accept to spend at least one hour per day time to gather data concerns property and share price variation, company's future development tend, the property's quality and the product's quality for their choices, they won't make without analysis of their choice product share or property before purchase. They have habits to gather any data to analyze their shares or properties purchase choice.

As my analysis indicates that discounted price may be poor long time. It's share price will have chance to be fallen down, because its product quality may be worse to compare its competitors. So, share investors ought consider the company's price whether has discount and how long time discount in order to decide to buy its shares. Also, as one property , its price has must discount and its discount period is long time. Then, the property invetor needs to consider whether this property's price will rise up easily, because it is common that consumers feel the property's quality is poor and it is not comfortable to live. Then, the property developer will reduce its property price to attract consumers to buy . Hence, it explains why some products need to be reduced their sale price, because those sellers feel their products will be difficult to sell, if they don't reduce their sale price. So, property or share consumers may have much power to spend per day some time to gather data and analyze and find reasons why their price will increase or decrease in order to make accurate purchase decision to create long time wealth income.

Hence, such as these both kinds of share investment and property product example, any one share or property consumer will have possible to be productive consumer, if he can accept to spend one to two houes per day time to carry on gathering data and comparing share or property market price variation analysis task. Then, they will have possible to earn extra more income.

How to create the bottom of the pyramid to the low income level consumer consumption desire

It has one interesting question to businessmen: How to create the bottom of the pyramid of the low income level consumer individual consumption desire? IN general, our society will feel difficult to persuade the low income level consumers to accept to buy the higher price and better quality of product, because their income level is low. It will influence their consumption desire to choose to buy any higher price and bette quality of product in difficulty.

To solve this exciting to low income level consumer consumption desire to choose choose to buy the higher price and better quality of product challenge. I shall make the core set of assumptions in our social consumption market. The assumptions may include: The poor group of consumer is not the higher price and better quality of product sellers' main target consumers, the low income people had no effort and have no use for the higher price and better quality of products and services that are sold in the developed markets in habit, it is only the developed markets appreciate and will pay for new technology, the low income level consumers can accept to use the old generation of cheaper and low technological products in habit, intellectual excitment is in the developed markets. It would be hard to recruit training, and motivate the higher price and better quality of product sale managers who want to spend time in creating a commercial infrastructure at the bottom of the pyramid to the low income level consumers group.

The higher price and better quality of product sale managers do not get excited with business challenges that have a humanitarian element to them. So, above of these assumptions have explained that why the higher price and better quality of products salespeople will feel difficult to persuade the low income level consumers to choose to buy their products in our society. But, it is nor represent that they have no any marke opportunity at the bottom of this pyramid to the low income level consumers group. I shall indicate these factors how can change the low income level consumers ' preference choice to make purchase decision making influence to high price and better quality of products behaviors.

The media innovation drivers factor: Increasing aspirations of people everywhere. The powerful role of TV and the internet media has genetrated all, but the most remote rural villages , advertisement, such as Chinese, India low income people who are living in remote rural villages. This unprecedented assess to information is creating an attractive desire among the poor to increase their consumption and improve their standards of living.

The low income level poor people pursue the improvement of quality of living, life enjoyment factor: If the poor are not able to meet their aspirations in rural communities. They will migrate to cities, creating an urban improving of quality of living pursuit.

The breakdown of rural village life and pursuit of knowledge systems, city improved city quality of life model, migraton and urbanization will be the low income level people's life dream. For india example, it already has 70 cities with more than one million people. To be sustainable, economic deveopment at the bottom must felloe a fundamentally different logic. Due to many low income level people hope the other high income level people feel that they have effort to become their same high income level social status in future one day. So , they will be encouraged to buy the higher price and better quality to use when they feel to earn more money and begin to prepare to live to cities to live from rural village location. Because when they begin to choose to buy the higher price and better quality of products to use. They will feel that they have better or higher social status (not the bottom of the social low income level group status) again. Hence, the media innovation and social status changing factors will have possibe to influence thw low income people to accept to choose to buy the higher price and better quality of products to use.

These drivers combine to suggest that a significant portion of important business opportunities to persuade the low income level consumers to choose to buy the higher price and better quality of products. Such as innovation can serve the bottom of pyramid. The starting assumption must be that serving the bottom of the pyramid is not about cheap and low quality products.

It is about bring together the best of technology and a global resource back to address local opportunity. It is about innovation within a clearly defined opportunity space: cost, quality , local knowledge and needs, manufacturing volume . So, it the product can be innovated by its technological quality to let the low income level consumers feel satisfactory. Then, they will be persuaded to choose to pay higher price to buy the innovated products more easily.

" Big data" platform factor: The " big data platforms" such as Google and Facebook are becoming dominant. Organizing information is not just about the world, but about consumers themselves behaviors. It reshapes a range of high price and low price products markets based on empowering a narrow set of corporate advertisers to influence high income level consumers to believe the product's price is exceed the normal market level. It is still reasonable to accept to buy from internet. E-commerce allows advertisers to offer products at different prices level, what economists explain price discrimination to extract the maximum price from each individual consumer. Such online price discrimination raises prices overall for consumers, when often hurting lower income and less technological knowledge households.

The product actual information between big data companies and the low income level consumers is easily converted into economic inequality, when on side of every online transaction has so much more knowledge about the other during bargaining.

The information in consumer market is driven by data mining and facilitied by online services, may be an additional significant cause of this overall increase in economic inequality. So, big data platforms facilitate advertisers engaging in user profiling that aid these higher price and better quality product companies in extracting the maximum profit possible from the high income level and low income both consumers in the overall economy.

In conclusion, advertisers can deliver ads not just to the users most likely to be interested in the product, but an tailor prices for individual consumers in ways that can maximize the purchase desires from each online purchase to charge easily. Consumers can be influenced and offered higher prices to charge easily. The online consumers do not knoe whether what the product's reasonable price is charged in the visiting shop or store. So , it explains that why online consumers can accept to pay higher price to buy the products because they won't feel need to find the actual store sold price to judge whether the online sale price is reasonable or not to compare the store sale price.

CHAPTER THREE

Exciting salespeople performance methods

Exciting salespeople sale skills to be raised, it can increase consumer number. Any organizations can let salespeople feel happy to sell their products. Then their sale performance will also raise. The question concerns that how to make them to feel happy to help the organization to sell their products? I shall explain some methods as below:

How to manage sales for predictable revenue? In order to hold salespeople sale psychology whether they feel happy or unhappy, executives need to understand the essential activities, sales managers must focus on to be analysts for change, foster continuous improvement and create a sales culture that drives results. Sale executives need to know how to achieve top objectives of sales management is to drive sales, capture new revenue and exceed monthly sales and margin objectives, e.g. performing sale straregy development with each salesperson on Monday morning at a minimum, and in a formal one-on-one meeting during the week;using strategy tools and questioning techniques to ensure the prospects are qualified and the strategy is valid; knowing the ratio between future values and future monthly quotos to raise sale opportunities; six month on-going sale plan aims to make sure there are coordinated to achieve sale to various market segments; developing on ongoing series of networking events to build market awareness in order to ensure all salespeople attend specific events involved in networking by salespeople to, understanding the market how to influence salespeople sale method to sale number, understanding trends and seeking some channels to raise additional sales opportunities; how to create trained or warm sale environment to let sales teams feel happy to sell.

How to design and utilize efficient control sale procedures? The sale cycle procedure may include these market activities, such as advertising, sales promotion, market research, physical distribution, pricing , sale place, sale staffs seeking. SO, any organizations need have good sale planning, direction and control of the personnel, selling activities of a business with including recruiting, selecting, training, rating, supervising, paying or reward system, motivating strategy , as all these tasks apply to the personnel sales-force.

The factors may influence salespeople psychology, they may include fair income reward system, or appreciation methods and sale career development plan to every salesperson. It aims to encourage them to achieve the highest sale effort. Anymore, methods to train sale managers have the right direction to guide, lead and motivate their salespeople, e.g. knowledge of salespeople psychology needs how to satisfy them, understanding why they choose to do or act themselves sale behaviors in order to improve their weakness to motivate salespeople to achieve company's sale target goal every month easily, e.g. raising profitability, sales volume, market share, growth and corporate image building raise clients' confidence to choose to buy this company's any products more easily.

The sales organization is required for the following purposes, they may include: enabling top-management, to devote to more time in policy making for the growth and expansion of business to divide and fix authority among the subordinates , so that they may shirk work, to avoid repetition of duties and functions, so that there may not be any confusion among them to locate responsibility of each and every employee , so that they can complete the whole work in stipulated time, if not then the particular person must be responsible, to establish the sales effort to enforce proper supervision of sales force.

What does the concept of salespeople replacement value mean? What is a sales force turnover management tool? Sales force turnover is defined as the rate at which salespeople leave an organizations, resignations, retirements or dismissals. So, if the organization can raise the sales force turnover ratio, because many salespeople can be promoted or the retirement, or the sales force turnover ratio raising reasons as well as they are not resignation or dismissal reasons. I believe that the organization ought have good sale environment and reasonable reward and welfare strategy to let its salespeople feel happy to help this company to sell its products every day.

However, sales management's actions have direct or indirect effects to impact on turnover. Direct effects may include the firm's firing or dismiss policy. The indirect effects on sale turnover may include new salesperon recruiting and selecting policies affect the quality and performance of the sale force as well as the speed at which salespeople are replaced. The same policies have an impact on the sales force turnover rate through the characteristics of the newly recurited salespersons and the promotion , training, retraining policies, support, supervision, compensation. ALl of those factors have an impact on salesperson's personal satisfaction or dissatisfaction absolutely. So, any sale organizations need to concern how and why whether any one of above these factors may influence their salespeople how to perform or act sale behaviors in order to excite their sale number more effective in long term.

How to achieve sale force management effectively? Sale management is one strategy to many organizations, because organizations expect their salespeople can only raise product sale number. So , they will consider whetther how to implement the sale management strategy to be the most suitable to themselves sale organizations in order to excite their sale teams to sell their products to achieve sale growth aim effectively. So for organization's long term sale growth development, it seems that one excellent sale management strategy can help the organization has stable sale number growth in long term possible.

However, the term " selling" includes a variety of sales situations and activities. For example, those sales positions where the sales representative is required primarily to deliver the product to the customer on a regular or periodic basis. The emphasis is this type of sales activity is very different to the sales position where the sales representative is dealing with sales of capital equipment to industrial purchasers. IN additions some sales representatives deal only in export markets whereas others sell direct to customers in their homes. So, sale organizations need to sell to local or overseas market as well as its target customer is businessmen or individual consumer or both in order to implement to choose their most suitable sale management strategy to train their salespeople more effective or achieving sale growth objective only. Because these its sale major target and where sale market place both factors will influence how it ought train its salespeople, so any organization's training method ought be influenced to change by whom is its major sale target and
where is its major sale market location factors.

How to know the psychology of salesmanship? WHen the organization can predict or find reasons to explain why its salespeople feel unhappy to help

this organization to sell its products. Then, it can attempt to improve its weaknesses in order to let its salespeople to feel more sale service satisfactory feeling to continue to help this organization to sell its products. THen, it won't need not often to train or recruit new salespeople to replace its old salespeople in consequence. How to know what its salespeoples' real need in order to raise their sale service satisfactory feeling ?

Psychology means that " science of the mind" and psychology plays to important part in business and it is quite worth to bring to influence any organization salespeoples' posivitive or negative sale emotion in their every sale process between themselves and their every client in personal. For example, if the salesperson often have negative emotion or he feels unhappy in every sale process, then he will encounter or increase many times of sale failure possibilities. He will feel that he is one poor verbal advertiser or seller or promotor to help his organization to promote its products to sell again as well as he will lose confidence to sell any products next sale chance, because his failure sale experiences are accumulated to influence his sale emotion to be poor or difficult sale.

Hence, the poor performance salesperson needs have more successful sale experiences to compensate his / her prior many sale failure times feeling, if the organization hopes this poor performance salesperson can raise sale number easily. Overall, any organizations need to concern how to improve or raise the more failure times of sale experience salespeoples' sale techniques or methods or attitudes more than choose to fire or dismiss them as well as finding another new salesperson to replace him/her. Because it is possible that the salesperson 's poor sale performance that is not due to himself/herself poor sale effort and sale knowledge or lacking sale experience to the product, it may be due to the poor sale team cooperation relationship , feeling poor or not comfortable sale physcial shop environment, poor sale manager and other salespeople working relationship, the sale manager lacks leadership effort, poor family relationship etc. external factors more than himself/herself personal poor or negative emotion or poor health etc. personal factors. Hence, the organization ought enquire him/her why he/she feels unhappy to sell its products and it needs to attempt to find methods to solve his/her challenges immediately. If his/her challenges can be solved. It is possible that his/her sale efforts can be also raised for. So, if the organization can know how to utilize positive sale emotion psychological methods to predict or know why and how every salesperson perform his/her sale behavior in whose daily sale tasks, then it can concentrate on implementing effective and the most suitable sale training to raise their sale abilities more easily.

However, the sale training may include: How to build or improve long term good salesperson and his/her customer sale service relationship between every salesperson and every client in every buying and selling cycle process, how to using right communicating styleds for better understanding every client's real needs, powers and negotiating, e.g. every salesperson needs to review why there are many clients do not choose to buy any products from his sale presentation or promotion, finding every time sale failure reasons can let the salesperson makes himself/herself sale failure reasons evaluation or judgement in order to find what is the major reason influences his/her sale failure, e.g. lacking product knowledge, he/she often let many clients to feel that he lacks patience to listen the client's enquiry or feedback, his sale presentation is not attractive to let many clients like to stay longer time to listen his sale presentation in whole sale process, the salesperson himself/herself emotion is negative and he /she can let many clients feel he / she is not happy or does not enjoy to sell this product from himself/herself face impression or sale behavior impression easily, lacking enough sale techniques to persuade his/her clients why he/she ought choose to buy this product in whole sale process etc. these factors may influence the salesperson's sale failure chance to be raised. Hence sales manager ought need to spend long time to meet the poor sale performance salesperson to discuess what his/her sale challenges are the most major to influence his/her every sale successful chance in order to improve his/ her sale performance more successfully.

IN conclusion, the reasons why salespeople often encounter sale failure possibilities. The factors may include these aspects, such as they lask the desire to help customers to make satisfactory purchase decisons, they only concern how to achieve sale final objective or aim only, it will cause clients feel they do not real concern their real needs. They only concern to sell the product in success. They do not know how to describe the product whether what characteristics or features it owns accurately in order to increase sale chance to persudade them to make final decision to by the product, they do not attempt to participate the whole sale process to help them to choose the most right product in order to satisfy their any purcahse needs, they ought avoid deceptive or manipulative influence tactics, avoid the use of high pressure sales techniques etc. Thus, if any organizations can spend time to investigate what factors cause why any one of salespeople choose perform his/her sale behavior often in order to know or understand their salespeople' sale psychology absolutely. Then, I believe that their sale number will only grown more easily.

How salespeople behaviors influence consumer psychology and behavioral relationship

Can every consumer himself/herself personal psychology influence whose consumption behavior how to do final purchase decision? Why and how can psychological factor influence consumer behavioral change? Must psychological factor be the major influence to cause any consumers to make final purchase decision? Can other factors influence psychological factor to influence consumers final purchase decision?

I shall indicate online shopping method, how online shopping consumers are influences to make final purchase choice from their psychological changing influence. In fact, it may have different factors to influence consumer behavior towards online shopping. Usually online buyers will choose to buy any things, when they stay at home in preference. They feel turn on home computer to shopping in preference, due to They feel turn on home computer to apply internet channel to buy any things will be more safe to compare to use public libraries, shopping centers, schools, office computers' internet to buy any things. It is one good example to explain why online shoppers usually like to buy any things to turn on home computer internet to spend much time to choose to buy any things. Safety feeling psychological factor is one important factor to influence online shoppers prefer to turn on home computer to apply internet channel to buy any things . It is possible that they feel public places' computers are Insafe and their visa cards personal data will be theft by any one easily.

Due to online shopping method has risk to bring any online shoppers' visa card personal data loss or theft. So, safety psychological factor will influence many online shoppers choose to apply internet transaction tool to buy any things at home. Unless, the online shopper has no computer at home or whose computer has no internet installation to his/her computer. Then, he/she only chooses to use public computer internet to buy any things. Hence, it explains that safety psychological factor can dominate or control any online shoppers' purchase behaviors to choose where is the most suitable place to use computer internet to carry on online shopping buying action. Also, it explains safety or privacy factor (avoiding visa card data theft) which will be one important factor to influence online consumers' preference purchase place choice (turning on the place's computer and applying its internet to carry on online shopping actions). Even, time factor and convenient both factors will not influence general online shoppers' using home computer and internet tool purchase behavior. For example, one student is staying at whose school library place at this moment, his school library's computer has installed internet too, he plans to buy one book for his reference at this moment. Although, he can apply this school library's computer internet to buy this book immediately. But, when he feels that he can buy this book immediately , if he decides to apply his school's library computer website to find any book shops , whether they have this book to sell to him. Possibly, he only needs to spend more ten minutes, or less than ten minutes to buy this book. SO, he does not need to spend longer time to catch any public transportation tools to go home and he also needs much time to turn on home computer to search any online book shops' websites to buy this book from himself home computer internet channel. However, it is due to privacy and safety psychological factor influence where is the most suitable place choice to buy this book from internet channel. SO, it explains that why psychological factor will be more important preference to compare time and convenient factors to influence online shoppers' (online shopping place) choice.

How psychological factor influences women /men (females/male) shopping place) choice. Shopper behavior has focuses on individuals and the factors that impact their decisions to spend their resources on consumption –related items. Female and male's consumption model or behavior has different, due to their sex is different. So, their psychology are also different to influence their shopping behaviors in possible. For example, women think differently from men because there are biological , neurological and behavioral variations between the brains of men and women . This differences in turn make an impact on their shopping behavior. When, men will load themselves with sufficient information of a product or service through internet, advertising, reviews. Otherwise, women would try to get benefit from others' shopping experience by asking peoples' ideas before they choose to buy any products.

Retail is the dominion of women and shopping is an action frequently seen as complementary to female role. IN general, female like to go to supermarkets, or any food shops to buy any kinds of food more than male. Women go on shopping to purchase both essential and discretionary products (daily living useful products), more than male. Females (women) are considered to be the most potential household consumers, as it has almost 80 percent of the domestic expenditure is spent by female to every householder (family member shoppers).

Any family member mother or sister will be the influential role. Female is the influential member , she can make final purchase decision in any householder (family) usually. It is possible due to any family member father or son has more confidence to believe mother or sister whose final purchase decisions are more accurate judgement before they pay to buy any things for home to use or eat. Hence, this female's accurate shopping judgement influence role or feeling which is one major psychological factor to explain that why householder female member can be the final shopping decision maker more than male member in any householder, because they are felt to be one confident home shopper to every male family member. In general, they are felt to make more reasonable or accurate judgement to buy any kinds of products or food for home to use or eat to compare male family members' shopping judgement.

Nowadays, it also explains why " confidence" is one important psychological factor to influence female, which is the major influential final shopping decision making more than male at any homes.

How can psychological factor influence either online or offline (visiting shops) shopping behavioral choice? Traditional shopping (visiting shops) had been one kind habitual consumption model or method, but internet shopping method had been also popular to be accepted to young people, e.g. student shoppers, even old people who also accepted to use internet to shopping. However, psychological factor is one important factor to influence their shopping method changing.

Online shopping is real fact in recent years. It will bring innovative and high technological shopping method to change traditional visiting shops shopping method as soon future. IN nowadays shopping environment, consumers like to buy any things conveniently in short time. Busy working and living factor influence their shopping feeling to be changed. IN general, consumers do not like to spend much time to visit any shops to choose any products and make final purchase decision. They like to make purchase decision in short time immediately. Due to internet is convenient, consumers they do no need to find where the shop can sell the product. They only need to turn on computer and enter any websites to search whether which online shop provides the kind of product to let them to bur from internet. Convenience and fun and high technological internet shopping method will be one kind of attractive shopping method to replace traditional visiting shops shopping method to change any one of consumers their traditional and habitual shopping model (method) or consumption behaviors daily.

The reason may be busy working time psychological factor to working people as well as busy learning time psychological factor to students. Convenient shopping factor, high technological invention of electronic shopping method factor. Many students and working people hope to spend less time to choose whether any product is the most suitable product to buy. They do not want to spend much time to search which shop can sell the product. Working and learning time is more important to compare shopping time. Hence time psychological factor will influence many young consumers choose to buy any things form internet channel. Otherwise, old people are retirement, they have much time to relax or entertain. SO, usually old people do not like to apply internet to buy any products at home. Because they have much time to visit any shops to go to shopping . Hence, psychological time factor will influence the shopping choice behavior difference between young age consumers and old age consumers.

Why can product knowledge psychological factor influence consumers product choice behavior? If the consumer feels the brand's any products have better to quality to compare other brands' products. He has confidence and product knowledge to use the brand's product. He has good past purchase experience to use the brand's products, because his useful feeling is good and he feels the brand's product can satisfy his need to use it. His past useful experience of this brand's product psychological factor will cause his future preference purchase choice , when he feels need to buy same or similar product in marketplace. So, it implies that when the consumer has good purchase and useful experience to the product, he will repeat to buy the brand's product again. Otherwise, when the consumer has bad purchase and useful experience to use the product before, he will lose confidence to buy the brand's product again. Hence, it explains why whether the consumer's good or bad purchase and useful experience psychological factor will influence whose purchase choice either repeat purchase or not repeat purchase again to the brand product.

Marketing message (unique value) and advertising campaigns influence psychological factor, it can influence consumers' confidence to use the brand's any products, even increase sales, because if the brand product seller can build good image to let consumers (public) to know its products existence by television, radio, newspapers, internet advertising channel. So, it seems that public advertisement promotion method can build good image to any product, it can achieve good image psychological factor to persuade any customers to attempt to buy the product to use or buy the food to eat. It is one building good image to let consumers to know the brand existence in the marketplace, it can bring message concerns that whether what kinds of products it is selling, how much price, discount it charges, what advantages of its products. All of these advertising message may persuade any customers to make first time purchase choice or repeat purchase decision, when they are watching its product advertisement from television, listening its advertisement from radio, reading its advertisement from newspapers or magazines etc. different advertisement channels in any time easily.

Any one of its advertisement message can let any audiences to remember the product's shape, color, size in their brains in long time. SO, long time advertisement memory to the product , it will bring positive consumption image influence to any audiences as well as persuading them to make final purchase choice to the product more easily.

Hence, advertising can shorten any consumers' purchase process or choice time to the product. Consumer behavior refers to the selection, purchase and consumption of products and services for the satisfaction of their wants. There are different processes involved in the consumer behavior. Initially the consumer tries to find what commodities, he would like to find what commodities, he would like to consume, then he selects only those commodities that promise greater utility. After selecting the commodities, the consumer makes an estimate of the available money which he spend. Lastly, the consumer analyzes the prevailing prices of commodities and takes the decision about the commodities he should consume usually. Hence, one attractive advertisement can influence many consumers feel that they do not need to spend much time to compare different kinds of similar products (product selection time), because the advertisement had attract their consideration to make final purchase decision. Hence, one attractive advertisement can shorten any consumers' (product selection time) to compare different kinds of products in order to make final purchase decision. Because it has build confidence to let many audiences feel the brand's products are worth to buy to compare other brand's products.

On conclusion, above these consumer behavioral purchase cases explain why consumer individual psychological factor can influence his/her final purchase decision. It implies that it has close relationship between consumer psychology and behavior. How the consumer's feeling to the product, it will cause his purchase behavior either selecting purchase it or selecting another product to replace it effect. SO, psychological factor is one absolute important factor to influence consumer behavior.

CHAPTER FOUR

Property seller sale skill training

Explaining clear property buyer contract agreement requirement
When one property seller can know whether the property sale contract how it can influence the property buyer to make property purchase decision, then he can sign the property property contract more easier immediately. The question is : How to persuade the property buyer to sign the property purchase contract immediately?
Any property seller needs to know whether the Standard Real Estate Contract content to every propety buyer. Because when the propety seller can know what the property purchase contract requirement between the propety buyer and him, he can explain the property contract content to let the property buyer to know clearly. Then, the property buyer may make the property purchase decision to sign the property contract to achieve the property sale transaction immediately.
Most people who are selling a home, condominium, townhouse, or other residential real estate will use a "standard" residential purchase and sale contract form (our form is one of several that are recognized in Florida for residential real estate transactions). These residential purchase and sale contract forms, once signed by the parties, becomes the document that governs their transaction. The contract, for instance, outlines what happens in the event of default by either the seller or the buyer (this is a term that can and should be negotiated between the parties — which is one more reason why it is so important to have a Florida real estate lawyer review your documents for you when you are buying or selling a house or condo here).

● Is a "Default" Defined in the Sales Contract?

How and when a seller defaults on a residential real estate contract is spelled out in the contract itself. Reading that paragraph to let the propery buyer to know, then the property buyer will find the following description of what happens when the Seller is in default of the contract as below:
SELLER DEFAULT: If for any reason other than the failure of Seller to make Seller's title marketable after reasonable diligent effort, Seller fails, neglects or refuses to perform Seller's obligations under this Contract, Buyer may elect to receive a return of Buyer's Deposit without thereby waiving any action for damages resulting from Seller's breach. Simply stated, the Buyer can ask for their deposit to be returned to them and then either sue the Seller for damages or seek to force the Seller to sell the property to the Buyer. (Note: If the Seller fails to "make title marketable after reasonable diligent effort," that is NOT considered a default.) So, the property seller needs explain whether how they property buyer can receive him deposit , when he ensures the property seller can not achieve the requirement in the sale contract after he paid the deposit to buy the property. It is one important factor to persuade the property buyer to sign the property sale contract because he will feel more confidence to pay back hid deposit if he ensures the property seller can not sell the property to him when he can not sell this property to follow the sale property contract requirement.
Sales contracts have time limitations within them; meaning, there is a deadline for things to occur, like the closing date. If the Seller does not deliver to the Buyer on the stated closing date a Deed, Bill of Sale, Closing Affidavit, and the other documents required under the Contract, then the Seller will be considered in default under the terms of the contract.mOther examples of a Seller default include:
Not allowing access to the property for inspections;
Not providing condominium documents to the buyer before the closing date; and
Not providing or disclosing material facts within the Seller's knowledge that affect the value of the Property and are not readily observable to the Buyer.

- How is a Breach of a Sales Contract Settled?

In instances where the Seller is in default as defined by the Default provision of the contract, what can the buyer do to settle the dispute? Again, the language of the contract itself will control what happens. In the form agreement referenced above, the parties agree to take their controversy to an alternative dispute resolution forum (aka mediation) before either party can file a lawsuit. The form contract also handles who pays what in fees and

expenses in mediation and any subsequent litigation.
Hence, if the property seller can explain whether how the property buyer can pay back his deposit after he sign the property sale contract. Then, he can persuade the property buyer to make decision to sign the property sale contract immediately.

Gathering property market inventory information

In any country property market, any kinds of property is same to inventory to any property sellers. So, any property agents need to spend time to gather his country's any kinds of property inventory information. It aims to compare whether what qualities and prices and living time and new or second hand property information, their locations are close to transport and shopping and leisure facilities etc. issues. They are different between the property agent's property inventory and his property agent competitors whose property inventory.
For a real estate agent to sell property, she must first have something to sell. That's where the Multiple Listing Service becomes a new agent's best friend. As soon as a newly licensed agent becomes associated with a real estate brokerage and joins the Multiple Listing Service, she has hundreds of listings she can sell. She can make appointments through the listing agents to show their houses. This is a great backup while she is working on listing her own properties. One of the first things a new agent should work on is putting together a great listing presentation to show to people who are thinking of selling property. The listing presentation shows what the agent will do to make sure the property is sold within a reasonable amount of time. That time frame depends on market conditions. The agent wants to convince the seller that she is an expert in her field, and if she's new, she can use the expertise of the company she is associated with. The listing presentation should be used on anyone who calls and wants to sell his property and on "For Sale by Owner" sellers. To sell property, the agent must establish an inventory. If an agent uses only the MLS, buyers will question her ability as an agent because she doesn't have her own inventory.

- Advertisement Property channels choice

Every real estate agent relies heavily on advertising the properties they have listed to get them sold. Advertisement may include: newspapers, magazine, TV, online, radio etc. advertise channel. So, any property agent needs to spend time to choose which advertise method is the best suitable channel to advertise their properties, then they need to spend time to decide how to design or perform their property advertise in order to attract many property buyers feel interest to choose their properties to buy. However, the most successful real estate agents market themselves more than they market the properties. If an agent gets the public to recognize his name or picture, people will already believe he is successful, and they will come to him.

A good agent will constantly be learning about his market and new real estate laws and guidelines, fast becoming an expert in the field. This is a highly competitive field, and agents must distinguish themselves among other agents. To do this, agents should market themselves with business cards and postcards with their pictures on them. Another tool many successful real estate agents use is establishing a quote or saying that people will remember them by. Marketing listings in real estate magazines, newspapers and postcards is an important function to get properties sold. Many agents will join organizations and put the organization's name on their signs. Special listings require special marketing, such as a custom sign or full-page ad. Agents do this to get the property sold, but they really want others who can't buy that property to remember their names. Selling property means agents need the buyers to come to them, even if the don't personally have the property they want listed.

Mechanics of Selling a Property how to carry on implementing the property agent sale steps in order to achieve the property sale aim to every property buyer. The steps may include as below:

The first step, an agent needs is a buyer. Once a buyer is interested, the agent writes a contract on the buyer's behalf and presents it to the seller. If the price and terms of the contract are acceptable to the seller, the seller will sign it. If they are not, then the seller can either reject the contract altogether or counter the buyer by changing the price and/or the terms and send it back to the buyer for negotiation. Once everything is agreed upon, the contract is signed buy both parties. The agent then guides the buyer through the process of financing, inspections, repairs and closing. The agent should attend the closing with the buyer to make sure everything goes according to plan and to make sure all the paperwork was prepared correctly. If a problem arises, the agent should handle it and do his best to get it resolved. A real estate agent does not get paid at the closing table. The commission is taken to the broker of the real estate company, and the agent is paid by the broker in accordance to their contract. If the property buyer's shopping for a new home and come across the one that fits you perfectly, the first thing the property agent wanst to do is get in touch with the real estate agent who's listed it. There are a number of ways to get this information, but the Multiple Listing Service isn't one of them. Detailed information in the MLS, like the listing agent's name and phone number, is available to licensed realtors only.

The second step, for a real estate agent to sell property, she must first have something to sell. That's where the Multiple Listing Service becomes a new agent's best friend. As soon as a newly licensed agent becomes associated with a real estate brokerage and joins the Multiple Listing Service, she has hundreds of listings she can sell. She can make appointments through the listing agents to show their houses. This is a great backup while she is working on listing her own properties. One of the first things a new agent should work on is putting together a great listing presentation to show to people who are thinking of selling property. The listing presentation shows what the agent will do to make sure the property is sold within a reasonable amount of time. That time frame depends on market conditions. The agent wants to convince the seller that she is an expert in her field, and if she's new, she can use the expertise of the company she is associated with. The listing presentation should be used on anyone who calls and wants to sell his property and on "For Sale by Owner" sellers. To sell property, the agent must establish an inventory. If an agent uses only the MLS, buyers will question her ability as an agent because she doesn't have her own inventory.

The third step, every real estate agent relies heavily on advertising the properties they have listed to get them sold. However, the most successful real estate agents market themselves more than they market the properties. If an agent gets the public to recognize his name or picture, people will already believe he is successful, and they will come to him. A good agent will constantly be learning about his market and new real estate laws and guidelines, fast becoming an expert in the field. This is a highly competitive field, and agents must distinguish themselves among other agents. To do this, agents should market themselves with business cards and postcards with their pictures on them. Another tool many successful real estate agents use is establishing a quote or saying that people will remember them by. Marketing listings in real estate magazines, newspapers and postcards is an important function to get properties sold. Many agents will join organizations and put the organization's name on their signs. Special listings require special marketing, such as a custom sign or full-page ad. Agents do this to get the property sold, but they really want others who can't buy that property to remember their names. Selling property means agents need the buyers to come to them, even if the don't personally have the property they want listed. Any property agent needs to solve these challenges , if they hope to achieve any successful property sale transaction easily.

How to Find Out the Listing Agent for an MLS
How to Get a Real Estate Market Analysis
How to Negotiate New Construction Homes in a Buyers' Market
Can You Use a Different Real Estate Agent After an Offer Was Declined?
How to Buy an Off Market Property
The Importance in Having a Professional Real Estate Agent
Do I Have to Pay a Real Estate Agent If I Change My Mind?
How to Find Out What Realtor Sold a House in My Neighborhood
What Can I Do With My Real Estate Broker's License?
Definition of a Real Estate Contract
How to Negotiate With a Realtor
How to List Your House With a Realtor
How do I Negotiate a Broker Listing Agreement?
Step-by-Step Real Estate Transaction
What Is a Buyer Specialist?
Who Pays Realtor Fees on Sale by Owner?
What Does Agent Owner Mean in Real Estate Listings?
How to Deal With Pushy Real Estate Agents
How to Sell an Unrenovated Old Apartment
How Much Money Does the Realtor Selling Your Home Get?

For example, if you're shopping for a new home and come across the one that fits you perfectly, the first thing you'll want to do is get in touch with the real estate agent who's listed it. There are a number of ways to get this information, but the Multiple Listing Service isn't one of them. Detailed information in the MLS, like the listing agent's name and phone number, is available to licensed realtors only.

What is the MLS?

The MLS is an enormous collection of databases used by real estate professionals to make information about their listings available to other realtors. Real estate agents also use it to shop other realtors' listings. It contains a lot of detailed information about each property as well as the listing agent's name and how to contact her.In the old days, realtors used to meet up to discuss their listings with each other and take fellow realtors on tours of their best listings. Realtors have to split their commissions if another real estate agent sells the property, but 50 percent of a quicker sale isn't a bad trade-off. Only licensed realtors have access to all of the information in the MLS. In a sense, the listings in it are confidential pitches to other realtors to cooperate and share the earnings for a mutually agreeable transaction.

What MLS Information is Available?

If you're not a licensed real estate agent, you can still make some use of the MLS. But the information you'll have access to is pretty limited. Follow these steps to access public information in the MLS:

Go to MLS.com and click on "Search Listings."

Click on the state where you want to find available properties.

Click on the area of the state you're interested in.

Click on the specific development or neighborhood within the area that you're interested in.

Now you'll be able to see all of the listings in that spot. They consist of one photo and a very short, simple description like "single-family home" or "vacant land." A few listings show the number of bedrooms, the number of baths and square footage, but that's it. Only about half show prices.

These days most of what's on the MLS's website is also on Zillow and Trulia. These are the two most popular real estate websites. Realtors know that a lot of people start shopping online so many put their properties on these websites. It's easy to find out who the listing agent is on Zillow and Trulia. For Zillow, simply click on the property , your property buyer has interested in, then click on the big blue "Contact Agent" button. A form opens up that not only gives your property buyer the listing agent's name, it also gives your property buyers his phone number and there's a thumbnail photo of him. If you want him to contact you, fill out the form and click on "Contact Agent" again.

For Trulia, the form is right on the main page of each listing below the property photos. From any page that has multiple property ads, click on the property you're interested in then scroll down a bit to the "Request Info" form. Below the red "Request Info" button you'll see a thumbnail of the listing agent. Hover your cursor over his photo and you'll get a pop-up with his name and phone number.

Alternatives for Finding Listing Agents

The fourth step , any property sell needs to know that your property buyers have alternatives to find any one listing agents. If the property your property buyer has interested in isn't on Zillow or Trulia, he can still find out who the listing agent is by driving over to the property. The listing agent's name and phone number will be on the for sale sign. Of course, this isn't practical if your property buyer considering a long-distance move, but if your property buyers have friends in the area, maybe they will do this for you. Additionally, some realtors erect outdoor brochure boxes on properties they're selling. These boxes hold flyers that give detailed information about the property, including who the listing agent is and how to contact them. So, you need prepare any attractive advertise to persuade or excite your potiential property buyers feel perfer to choose your property agent sale service from listing agents. If your advertise can attract their attention, then they will feel prefer to choose to find your property agents to help them to choose any property to buy among many property agents in your country. One last thing – if the property is advertised on Craigslist it should have the listing agent's name and contact information in the ad. But sometimes they only give the name of the real estate company. If you see an ad like that just call the company and ask whose listing it is. Happy new home hunting!

You need to let your property buyers feel that you have effort to help your property buyers to set the reasonable value for their property choices. An successgul property agent needs to know what his job responsibility and he needs to attempt to improve his property sale method or skill in order to acheive to let any potential property customers have more satisactory feeling after he explains any kinds property information to let them to know clearly.

An estate agent will be able to give your property buyers to feel you have an expert view on how much your house is worth, setting it at the right price to market. They will draw upon their knowledge of the local property market as well sold prices of other local homes like yours from the Land Registry to give you an accurate picture of what homes like yours are selling for and why you might pitch for more or less.

It is important to do your research first so you have a figure in your mind. To do this, start by getting a free online instant valuation and by checking Land Registry figures. Then get three different estate agent valuations as some firms may use the strategy of over-estimating the price of your home to try to secure you as a client. A good agent will have experience of what features buyers in the area are looking for and be able to tell you whether it is worth making changes to improve the appeal of your home to achieve a higher price. They should be able to impress you with their local knowledge and expertise in selling houses like yours.

You also need to know your property buyers can choose to buy house from online channel. If they are considering using an online estate agent, it is still a good idea to get three valuations from high street firms because online agents tend to lack knowledge of the local market and will therefore be heavily reliant on online data to carry out their valuations. So, you may choose to design your property online website to provide colorful and beautiful house photos in order to attract their consideration. So, online sale channel is also important to excite your property buyers' choices from your property sale service.

The fifth step, you need to judge whether your property buyer's property purchase desire is how much as well as you need to arrange any follow services to satisfy their property service needs. When you are such as an estate agent , you should arrange for your property to be professionally photographed, get an accurate floor plan drawn up and write a detailed, accurate, attractive description of your home to be used in the brochure, its shop window and on the big property portals.

You shouldn't have to pay any extra for the photography and these other basics as they should all be included in the % fee the estate agent charges for marketing and selling your home. Make sure that the pictures are up to scratch as they are crucial to attract plenty of viewings. If they are not up to scratch, request that new ones are taken. And cast your eye over the property details. These need to be correct to avoid problems further down the line. You are such as an estate agent will be able to tell you how the big property websites work – such as Rightmove and Zoopla – and have accounts with them so that your property will be advertised on these sites.

Before you start marketing your home it is a legal requirement to have an Energy Performance Certificate (EPC) which tells potential buyers how information about a property's energy use and typical energy costs. Your home will be given an energy efficiency rating from A (most efficient) to G (least efficient) and the EPC is valid for 10 years. Your estate agent can organise this for you for a fee. Get a quote from your estate agent but shop around. You can find an assessor and get a quote here. If you have purchased your home in the last 10 years you may already have a certificate which is still valid. You need to know that your property buyers will attempt to find and compare local estate agents based on how often they achieve asking price, how long it takes them to sell and their success rate

Conduct viewings

The six step, you need to know how to conduct your viewings to let your property buyers feel satisfaction to your property sale introduction service.

You will arrange viewings of your property buyer's choice of home and guide your potential buyers around the property answering any questions or queries people have. You should also make sure your property buyer is secure when they leave after a viewing.
Once your client's property is on the books with another estate agent they may have a list of potential buyers who have expressed an interest in a property like yours that they will call to market your home to. Hence, you need to know how to let your property buyers feel your property inventory is better than your other property agents when you invite your property buyer to view your property inventory in the first time.
Estate agents may also arrange an open house for their property where numerous buyers visit during a specific time period. You need to let your property buyer to feel that you can give the advantage of using your estate agent service to let him to conduct viewings on your behalf is they are seen as a more neutral party by potential buyers who may ask them questions that they would be embarrassed to ask the owner themselves. It also takes the hassle away of you having to show people round your home. If you conduct your viewings yourself, you need to ask yourself how the estate agent is earning their commission fee.
In this instance, you might be better off selling with an online estate agent. You usually pay a fixed fee (which works out cheaper than the percentage commission fee high street agents charge) but is payable upfront i.e. whether you sell your property or not. The default option with online estate agents is that you show potential buyers around the property yourself. Hybrid estate agents like PurpleBricks are growing in popularity as they also offer a local property expert to conduct viewings for you. Other online estate agents are increasingly following suit by offering add-on options to conduct viewings. But these usually come at an additional charge – so speak to the agent to understand how many viewings are included, what the additional price is, who will conduct the viewings and how it will work in practice. You need to attempt to find and compare online estate agents, their packages and fees before you decide to implement online property sale platform.

Manage negotiations

The final step, you need to know how to mange negotiaton between you and your any one property buyer. A key part of an estate agent's job is to manage negotiations and act as a go-between for any potential buyers and the owner of a property. Offers should be made to the estate agent who will pass them on to the owner and, similarly, relay the seller's response to any offer submitted.

During this period the estate agent can be helpful to the buyer but ultimately they should always put the seller, their client, first and aim primarily to get them the best price for the property. If your propety buyers are thinking about making an offer on a property , you need to know your property buyer can ask the another estate agent for more information on the position of the owners – have they found their dream home and are they in need of a quick sale, or do they need someone who is prepared to wait while they hunt for somewhere to live? Buyers can also usually get a feel for what level of offer might be considered acceptable by the vendor via the estate agent.

Under the Property Ombudsman Code of Practice, estate agents must take reasonable steps to find out from the buyer the source and availability of their funds for buying the property and pass this information to the seller. This will cover whether the buyer needs to sell a property, requires a mortgage, claims to be a cash buyer or any combination of these. Usually they will ask the buyer to show an agreement in principle from a mortgage lender to prove that they are in a position to afford the property. Find out more with our guide to proof of funds.

Under this Code estate agents are also legally obliged to put all offers through to their client, you the seller, even if the buyer hasn't been financially qualified at this stage. When you accept an offer, it is then the estate agents job to regularly monitor the buyer's progress in achieving the funds required and keep you informed. All of this information will help your estate agent advise you on the position of the buyer and how serious or good an offer is. They should be able to help you decide whether or not to accept an offer – but ultimately that decision is up to you.

In final, Once your property buyer had accepted an offer, or had an offer accepted, then the estate agent should issue a Memorandum of Sale to the vendor, buyer and their solicitors all the information they need on each other and each party's solicitors. Many people think an estate agent's job ends once an offer has been accepted, but this is where a good estate agent will really come into their own by helping make sure that the offer moves forward, unblocking issues up and down the chain and working to the critical points of exchange of contracts and a date for completion. During this period your estate agent can act as your adviser and agony aunt as you negotiate the peaks and troughs of the sales process. You can lean on them as much or as little as you want.

Choosing the right estate agent

To achive any property sale success, you need to know how to attract any one property buyer to choose your property sale service in preference. When choosing an estate agent don't just go with whoever says they can sell your home for the highest price, or the agent with the lowest fee

Printed by Libri Plureos GmbH in Hamburg,
Germany